Danton's Death

Georg Büchner (1813–37) is one of the forefathers of twentieth-century theatre. He was born near Darmstadt in Germany and studied natural science at Strasbourg University and then at Giessen. Caught up in revolutionary activity he had to flee Germany in 1835, never to return. Although he died of typhus before his 24th birthday, he left three plays, all of which remained unperformed until the turn of the century, as well as a short novel, *Lenz*, and a revolutionary pamphlet urging peasant revolt. Of the three plays *Danton's Death* (1835; first staged 1902), set during the French Revolution, anticipates modern epic theatre, *Leonce and Lena* (1836; first staged 1895) is an absurdist comedy, and *Woyzeck* (1836; first staged 1913) foreshadows both naturalism and expressionism.

Howard Brenton was born in Portsmouth in 1942. His many plays include *Christie In Love* (Portable Theatre, 1969); *Revenge* (Theatre Upstairs, 1969); *Magnificence* (Royal Court Theatre, 1973); *Brassneck*, with David Hare (Nottingham Playhouse, 1973); *The Churchill Play* (Nottingham Playhouse, 1974; twice revived by the RSC, 1978 and 1988); *Short Sharp Shock*, with Tony Howard (Royal Court and Stratford East, 1980); *Bloody Poetry* (Foco Novo, 1984, and Royal Court Theatre, 1987); *Weapons Of Happiness* (National Theatre, 1976; winner of the Evening Standard Award 1976); *Epsom Downs* (Joint Stock Theatre, 1977); *Sore Throats* (RSC, 1978); *The Romans In Britain* (National Theatre, 1980; revived Sheffield Crucible Theatre 2006); *Thirteenth Night* (RSC, 1981); *The Genius* (Royal Court, 1983); *Pravda*, with David Hare (National Theatre, 1985; winner of the Evening Standard Award, 1985); *Greenland* (Royal Court, 1988); *Iranian Nights* with Tariq Ali (Royal Court Theatre, 1989); *Moscow Gold*, with Tariq Ali (RSC Barbican Theatre, 1990); *Berlin Bertie* (Royal Court, 1992); *Ugly Rumours*, with Tariq Ali (Tricycle Theatre, 1998); *Collateral Damage* with Tariq Ali and Andy de la Tour (Tricycle Theatre, 1999); *Kit's Play* (RADA Jerwood Theatre, 2000); *Snogging Ken*, with Tariq Ali and Andy de la Tour (Almeida Theatre, 2000); *Paul* (National Theatre 2005; nominated for the Olivier Award, 2006) *In Extremis* (Shakespeare's Globe, 2006/7); *Never So Good* (National Theatre, 2008) and *Anne Bolyn* (Shakespeare's Globe, 2010). He wrote the libretto for Ben

Mason's football opera *Playing Away* (Opera North and Munich Biennale, 1994; revived Bregenz Festival, 2007) and a radio play, *Nasser's Eden* (1998). Versions of classic texts include *The Life Of Galileo* (1980) and an earlier version of *Danton's Death* (1982), both at the National Theatre, and Goethe's *Faust* (RSC 1995/6). He wrote a stage adaptation of Robert Tressell's *The Ragged Trousered Philanthropists* (Liverpool Everyman and Chichester Festival 2010). His work for television includes *Dead Head* (a four-part serial for BBC2, 1986) and thirteen episodes of the first four series of *Spooks* (Kudos/BBC1,2001–05; BAFTA Best Drama Series 2003).

Georg Büchner

Danton's Death

in a new version by Howard Brenton

from literal translations by Jane Fry and Simon Scardifield

B L O O M S B U R Y

LONDON • NEW DELHI • NEW YORK • SYDNEY

Bloomsbury Methuen Drama

An imprint of Bloomsbury Publishing Plc

50 Bedford Square	1385 Broadway
London	New York
WC1B 3DP	NY 10018
UK	USA

www.bloomsbury.com

Bloomsbury is a registered trade mark of Bloomsbury Publishing Plc

This new version of *Danton's Death* first published in 2010, from a literal
translation by Simon Scarfield, based on the version published in 1982
by Methuen London Ltd, from a literal translation by Jane Fry.

Original work entitled *Dantons Tod*

© Howard Brenton 2010

Visit www.bloomsbury.com to find out more about our authors and their books
You will find extracts, author interviews, author events and you can sign up for
newsletters to be the first to hear about our latest releases and special offers.

British Library Cataloguing-in-Publication Data
A catalogue record for this book is available from the British Library.

ISBN: PB: 978-1-4081-3283-8
EPDF: 978-1-4081-3559-4
EPUB: 978-1-4081-3560-0

Library of Congress Cataloging-in-Publication Data
A catalog record for this book is available from the Library of Congress.

Danton's Death

Introduction

Karl Georg Büchner was born in Goddeau, a village near
Darmstadt, on 17 October 1813, the eldest of six children. It was a
respectable family with a medical tradition; his father was an
eminent doctor and a staunch royalist. When he was three the
family moved to Darmstadt. Georg's childhood was idyllic: his father
encouraged the boy's fascination with the natural world, giving him
a scientific precision in the way he looked at things, while his mother
gave him a love of poetry, fairy tales and folk song. The forensic
intensity of his mature writing, which at any moment can soar into
wildly imaginative imagery, was clearly influenced by his parents'
enthusiasms. The decent, bourgeois couple cannot have realised
they were laying the seeds for two of the greatest revolutionary
works in European theatre: *Woyzeck* and *Danton's Death*.

Büchner was a diffident schoolboy. He found the education
stifling, scribbling on one of his school books: 'Oh for something
alive! What's the good of this deadwood?' Then in July 1830 a
Revolution broke out in France. The Bourbon King Charles X was
overthrown. For three days Paris relived the street fighting, the
political turmoil, the passion and the fear of the First French
Revolution of 1789. The sixteen-year-old Büchner's imagination
was fired. In an essay of 1830 he wrote that the French Revolution
was a 'Just war of extirpation, revenging the abominations which
infamous despots have inflicted on mankind for centuries'.

Six months after leaving school he went to Strassburg, then a French
city, to study medicine. He threw himself into the cosmopolitan
student world, made many friends in literary and political circles and
fell in love with Wilhelmine ('Minna') Jaegle, the daughter of his
clergyman landlord. They were happy days for the neurotic, rather
sickly but attractive young man in flight from a stuffy provincial
world. He and Minna became secretly engaged. She was the only
woman in his life and, after his early death, she never married.

But after two years in Strassburg (1831–33) Büchner had to move
to the small university of Giessen in Germany in order to qualify as
a doctor. After the light and freedom of Strassburg he found Giessen
grey and stifling. The Grand Duchy of Hessen Darmstadt was a
small independent Princedom, still feudal and absolutist – Germany
was not united until the 1860s. The realities of life amongst the
peasantry in his homeland shocked the young, would-be

revolutionary. The price of corn was falling and taxes were being driven up. Starvation was rife. Any protests were brutally put down by the military. Büchner tried to shut out the reality, reading 'medicine by day and history and philosophy by night', but did not succeed. 'The political state of affairs drives me mad', he wrote to a friend. 'The poor patiently pull the cart on top of which the princes and the educated act out their bizarre comedy'.

In April of 1833 students led an armed uprising in Frankfurt on Maine. It failed. But Büchner was wholly in sympathy. He became convinced that only force could advance the progressive cause. The abortive Frankfurt coup encouraged activists in Giessen and Büchner joined them. He became friendly with Ludwig Weidig, a political progressive but also a devout Christian. Büchner was an atheist but Weidig had something he wanted: a secret printing press. He would write a pamphlet addressed directly to the peasantry encouraging revolution 'from below'. In March 1834 he persuaded Weidig to print *Der Hessische Landbote* (*The Hesse Country Messenger*). Brilliantly written in impassioned but simple language, it began with the inflammatory words: 'Peace to the hovels! Death to the Palaces!'.

As the English poet Shelley found, with a similar enterprise in Dublin, the poor do not necessarily take kindly to young intellectuals exhorting them to rebellion with pamphlets. The campaign was a disaster. The peasants were frightened and handed over copies to the police – subversion was treason and harshly dealt with. At the same time Büchner started a Society For Human Rights, a radical revolutionary cell with working-class as well as middle-class members – a dangerous and illegal enterprise in semi-feudal Giessen. In September 1834 Büchner had a second batch of *The Messenger* printed. But the copies were found in the possession of a friend who was arrested. Büchner's room was raided in his absence and he narrowly escaped arrest himself.

Railing against the 'vile mentality' of the peasantry, Büchner fled to Darmstadt for protection in his father's house. Horrified, his father demanded he concentrate solely on his medical studies. There, in less than five weeks in January and February of 1935, Büchner wrote *Danton's Death*. He did so in the greatest secrecy, writing on his dissecting table so he could hide the manuscript beneath medical books when his father came into the room. He was under terrible pressure: the police called him in repeatedly for interrogation. On 9 March, with the play finished, he fled to

Strassburg, rather than face arrest. A warrant against him was issued on 9 June and for the rest of his life he was in danger of being sent back to Germany on charges of subversion and treason.

Danton's Death has a strong sense of authenticity. Büchner knew the speeches of the revolutionary leaders by heart and whole sentences of the text are verbatim. But the play goes way beyond historical 'realism'. It gives us direct access to what Danton, Robespierre and their followers actually felt, to their secret and darkest thoughts during the desperate days of the French Terror in 1794. Perhaps Büchner's visceral sense of the Revolutionary leaders' predicament comes from his own: those days of heightened awareness under surveillance and in fear of arrest in his father's house. The play is also profoundly paradoxical. It is a political tragedy which is remorselessly frank about the horrors of the Terror. It could easily be used by the right for sermons about the dangers of the left. Yet it communicates a strange sense of beauty, even hope: that the enterprise that killed Danton and two and a half thousand others on the guillotine, was nevertheless worthwhile. Against all the odds it is a revolutionary play.

In exile in Strassburg Büchner worked hectically. He lived off the proceeds of two translations of plays by Victor Hugo. His father, though stricken with worry, always supported him financially. Büchner sent *Danton's Death* to a well known German literary figure, Karl Gutzkow, who immediately recognised its genius and arranged publication in July of 1835 – it was heavily censored and the only work by Büchner published in his lifetime. In the autumn of 1835 he wrote his novel *Lenz* and worked on a treatise concerning the nervous system of fish, a subject on which he gave three lectures at the Association of Natural Sciences in Strassburg. He began work on his fairy-tale play *Leonce and Lena* and worked on *Woyzeck*, which remained unfinished at his death. His medical lectures were much admired and he was awarded a Doctorate of Philosophy by the University of Zurich. He moved there in October 1836 and lectured on 'The Nerves of The Cranium'.

On 27 January 1837 he wrote to Minna in high spirits: 'I don't feel like dying and I'm in as good health as ever . . . Addio, piccola mia!'

On 2 February he fell ill. He had typhoid. Minna rushed from Strassburg to his sickbed but he died on 19 February, 1837. He was twenty-three years and four months old. 'Information for this article was included in a programme note by Hugh Rank for the National Theatre's 1982 production of Danton's Death'.

Howard Brenton, 2010
Commissioned by the National Theatre, June 2010

This version of *Danton's Death* was first performed in the Olivier Theatre at the National Theatre on 15 July 2010. The cast was as follows:

Georges Danton	Toby Stephens
Legendre	Ashley Zhangazha
Camille Desmoulins	Barnaby Kay
Lacroix	Gwilym Lee
Hérault-Séchelles	Max Bennett
Julie, *Danton's wife*	Kirsty Bushell
Lucile, *Desmoulins' wife*	Rebecca O'Mara
Marion, *a prostitute*	Eleanor Matsuura
Robespierre	Elliot Levey
Saint-Just	Alec Newman
Barère	Phillip Joseph
Collot d'Herbois	Chu Omambala
Duplay, *Robespierre's landlady*	Judith Coke
Eléonore, *Duplay's daughter*	Rebecca Scroggs
Elisabeth, *Duplay's daughter*	Elizabeth Nestor
Herman *President of the Revolutionary Tribunal*	Michael Jenn
General Dillon, *prisoner in the Conciergerie*	David Beames
A Lyonnais	Ilan Goodman
Citizens	Stefano Braschi
	Jason Cheater
	Emmanuella Cole
	Taylor James
	David Smith
	Jonathan Warde

Director   Michael Grandage
Designer   Christopher Oram
Lighting Designer   Paule Constable
Music and Sound   Adam Cork

Characters

Georges Danton
Legendre
Camille Desmoulins   *Dantonists*
Lacroix
Hérault-Séchelles

Julie, *Danton's wife*
Lucile, *Desmoulin's wife*

Marion, *a prostitute*

Robespierre
Saint-Just   *Members of the Committee*
Barère   *of Public Safety*
Collot d'Herbois

Duplay, *Robespierre's landlady*
Eléonore
  her daughters
Elisabeth

Herman, *President of the Revolutionary Tribunal*
General Dillon, *a prisoner in the Conciergerie*

A Lyonnais
A Jacobin
Three Prisoners
A Warder
Three Citizens

Frequenters of the Palais Royale, members of the Jacobin Club, members of the National Convention

Act One

Scene One

A private room in the Palais Royale. **Men** *and* **Women** *at a card table. Other* **Men** *and* **Women** *drinking, embracing.*

Danton *and* **Julie**. *He is sitting at her feet.*

Julie Darling Georges, do you trust me?

Danton How can I tell? We're lumbering, thick-skinned animals. Our hands reach out to touch, feel, but the strain's pointless. All we can do is blunder around, rubbing our leathery hides up against each other. We're very much alone.

Julie But you know me, Danton.

Danton I know your dark eyes, your curly hair, your fine skin and that you call me 'darling Georges'. But! (*He points to his forehead and eyes.*) Here, here, what lies behind here? Our senses are crude. We'd have to crack open our skulls to know each other, tear out each other's thoughts from the fibre of the brain.

Camille Desmoulins, **Lacroix** *and* **Hérault-Séchelles** *come on.*

Lacroix? Why look so grim? Have you lost your red revolutionary cap? Did St Jacques of the Jacobins give you a nasty look? Or did it just rain at the guillotining?

Camille He's parodying Socrates! Oh you clever, clever, classical revolutionaries, so romantic about Greeks and Romans. You need a dose of our Romantic guillotine. That will bring you back to reality.

Lacroix Twenty more executions today. Why doesn't it stop? We had to put the Girondins on trial, they were in league with aristocrats. And we agreed with Robespierre, he was right to demand that the Committee of Public Safety send Hébert and his Leftists to their deaths. Hébert was too extreme, too impetuous, his were the politics of anarchy.

But now there's no threat from Right or Left, the danger's gone: so why are we still killing each other?

Hérault Because Robespierre and his clique want to take us back to some kind of bloodsoaked Eden. First Saint-Just wants us crawling on all fours like babies, then Robespierre wants us sat on school benches while he drums catechisms into us about a Supreme Being, concocted from the crackpot theories of a Swiss philosopher with a mind like a clockmaker.

Lacroix Strange how Jean-Jacques Rousseau actually believed in human innocence.

Hérault In politics ideas of innocence can kill.

Lacroix So must we be dirty and bloody as newborn children forever, with coffins for cradles and severed heads for toys?

Camille We have reached a moment of transformation. The Revolution must end, the Republic must begin.

Hérault Yes! In the constitution of our state, rights must replace duties.

Camille Yes! The well-being of the individual must replace the vile idea of public virtue.

Danton (*heard by* **Julie** *but not the others*) Must, must . . .

Hérault We must be free to speak our minds and act according to our natures. It's no concern of the state whether we're wise or stupid, good or bad. We are all fools, we've no right to force our follies on each other. We must claim the right to enjoy life in our own way, with this one rule: no one may enjoy themselves at another's expense, or stop another's pleasure.

Camille The state must be a transparent robe, clear as water, that clings closely to the body of the people. Every ripple of the sinews, every tensing of the muscles, every swelling of the veins must be imprinted upon its form. Let our dear sinner-girl, France, be as she is.

And give us naked gods, Bacchus-loving women. We don't want to stop Robespierre's virtuous Romans from sitting in their corner, cooking their turnips. We just want to stop them giving us gladiatorial bloodbaths.

Let the divine Epicurus, the philosopher of pleasure, and Venus with her lovely arse, be the doorkeepers of our Republic. Not Saint-Just and Saint Robespierre.

Danton. You will launch the attack in the Convention.

Danton I will, you will, he will. 'If we live to see day dawn', as the old women say. Here's something to think about: in one hour's time, sixty minutes will have passed.

Camille Something of a crushingly obvious remark, Danton . . .

Danton Oh everything is obvious, no? For example, who will put this visionary splendour into practice?

Lacroix We will. And all decent people.

Danton Ah! That 'and', a long word, it sets us and 'decent people' far apart. The road is long, will the 'decent' be there with us at its end? I think not, they'll have run out of puff a long way back. You can lend money to 'decent people', marry your daughters to them, but that's all they're good for.

Camille If you don't believe in decency, why begin the struggle at all?

Danton Oh understand me, I too find Robespierre and his sanctimonious, jumped-up, would-be Romans repulsive. Whenever I see them I want to kick them in the teeth. But that's just me.

He rises.

Julie Are you going?

Danton (*to* **Julie**) Yes I'm off. They make me sick with their politics.

As he leaves.

Parting words. A prophecy: the statue of freedom has not yet been cast, the furnace is red hot, we too may yet burn our hands.

He goes off.

Camille   Let him go. Do you think he'll keep his hands off, when the time comes?

Scene Two

Robespierre*'s lodgings, 366 Rue Saint-Honoré. A full-length mirror.* **Robespierre,** *his landlady* **Madame Duplay** *and her daughters* **Eléonore** *and* **Elisabeth**.

Robespierre   I must go to the Jacobin Club at once.

Duplay   What happened?

Eléonore   We were in the street. Suddenly they were all around us . . .

Elisabeth   It was a mob!

Robespierre (*taking off his coat. They help him dress.*) Madame Duplay, if I may trouble you, the cream waistcoat.

Elisabeth   They were chanting death to 'those who read and write'. And they were dragging a young man along, his face was bloody and I think his arm was broken, they shouted he was an aristo and they were going to hang him from a lantern! It was horrible.

Eléonore   The anger of the starving.

Duplay   Citizen, they could have killed you.

Robespierre   I have nothing to fear from the people. The green coat.

Eléonore   And you walked straight into the crowd and said 'only in the name of the law'. A drunken brute shouted 'what's the law?'. You looked him in the face and said . . .

Robespierre   'The will of the people, that is the law.' The other wig.

Elisabeth   Then someone shouted that the September massacres hadn't been enough, a few aristocrats and priests killed in the prisons, they needed more blood, that the guillotine's too slow and we need a downpour and for a moment I thought they were going to kill us . . .

Robespierre   Then you, my dear Eléonore, kindly introduced me to our fellow citizens.

Eléonore   Silence for the incorruptible! Listen to the Messiah, sent to elect and judge. Silence for Robespierre.

Robespierre *is now dressed.* **Duplay** *hands him his walking cane.*

And you said 'poor virtuous people . . . '

Robespierre   'Poor virtuous people. You do your duty, you sacrifice your enemies. People, you are great, amid flashes of lightning and peals of thunder, you reveal yourself. But, good people, do not wound your own body, do not murder yourself in your rage. You are strong, only by your own self-destruction can you fall. Your enemies know that. But your lawgivers keep watch. Their eyes are infallible, they guide your hands and from the hands of the people there can be no escape. Go to the Jacobin Club. Meet me there. I open my arms to you, we will put your enemies on trial for their lives.'

Elisabeth (*overcome*)   The power of words.

Duplay   Long live Robespierre!

Eléonore   Long live Robespierre!

Robespierre *catches sight of himself in the mirror. He touches his face.*

Scene Three

The Jacobin Club.

A Lyonnais   Fellow Jacobins. We, your brothers from Lyons, pour out the bitter anger in our hearts. Our city is still in the grip of enemies of the Revolution: Girondins, so-called moderates, aristocrats in disguise still rule. They guillotined our leader, Joseph Chalier, and the blade was blunt, four times it fell on the neck of that hero of the people! And his murderers still walk the earth as if they will never lie in a grave. Why don't you act? Have you forgotten that Lyons is a stain on the ground of France that must be blotted out by the corpses of traitors? That Lyons is the whore of kings and can only wash away her sores in the waters of the Rhone? Your mercy murders the Revolution. Every breath an aristocrat draws is the death rattle of liberty. Only a coward dies for the Republic, a Jacobin kills for it! Know this, if you falter, there is only one choice for the Jacobins of Lyons: Cato's dagger – patriotic suicide.

Applause and confused shouts. Enter **Robespierre**.

A Jacobin   We'll drink hemlock with you like Socrates!

Legendre (*quickly climbs up onto the platform*)   No need to look as far as Lyons. They who wear silk coats and trousers, who drive in coaches, they who sit in the boxes of theatres and talk like the Dictionary of the Academy, still find their heads stuck firmly on their necks. Now they joke and say 'let's give Chalier and Marat a double martyrdom and guillotine their statues!'.

Violent commotions in the Club.

Collot d'Herbois   And I ask you, Legendre, how do you dare speak such thoughts? We know who your friends are. It's time to tear off the masks. The Committee of Public Safety has a better grasp of logic, Legendre! Don't worry. The statues of the Revolution's saints are safe. Like Medusa's head, they will turn traitors to stone.

Robespierre   I demand to speak.

Jacobins   Silence! Silence for the Incorruptible!

Robespierre   We waited only for this cry of outrage before
we spoke. Our eyes were open, we saw the enemy advance
but we did not sound the alarm, we let people keep watch
and they did not sleep, they reached for their weapons. We
flushed the enemy from hiding, we forced him to show
himself, now you see him in the clear light of day, now
you can cut him down, you have only to look at him and
he is dead.

I told you once before, understand. Yes yes, we beheaded a
king, destroyed the Girondins and royalists. But now we
face a greater danger: now the enemies of the Republic are
in two factions, two camps. Under banners of different
colours, by different routes, they scurry toward the same
goal. Yes yes, one of these factions is destroyed. In their
arrogance, their conceited madness, Hébert and his Leftists
declared war on the deity and on private property, but their
violent excess was a diversion to help the kings. They
parodied the lofty drama of the Revolution in order to
discredit it. Hébert's success would have tipped the
Republic into chaos, to the delight of the despots. Well, the
sword of the law has fallen on that traitor. But does that
worry the foreigners? No, why should it when there are
criminals of another kind to work for them? We have
achieved nothing for we have yet another faction to destroy.
It is the opposite of the first. It wants to make us weak. It's
battlecry is 'Mercy!'. And its tactic? To take away the
weapons of the people and the strength of the people and
deliver them, naked and cowed, into the hands of the kings
of Europe. The weapon of the Republic is terror. The
strength of the Republic is virtue. Virtue because without it
terror withers away; terror because without it virtue is
powerless. Terror is a by-product of virtue, it is nothing less
than swift, stern and unbending justice. People say that
terror is the weapon of tyranny, and that our government
therefore resembles a tyranny. Of course it does. But only in

as much as the sword in the hand of a fighter for freedom resembles the sword of a slave, fighting for a king. The despot rules his bestial serf through terror. As a despot he has that right. You are the founders of the Republic. You have the right to use terror to crush the enemies of liberty. The revolutionary government is the despotism of liberty against tyranny.

'Have mercy on the royalists!' some shout. Mercy for criminals? No! Mercy for the innocent, mercy for the weak, mercy for the unfortunate, mercy for mankind. The protection of society is only for the peaceful citizen. In a republic only republicans are citizens; royalists and foreigners are enemies. To punish the oppressors of mankind is a privilege; to pardon them, barbarism. Any sign of false compassion is a sign of hope for England and Austria.

And now, not content with disarming the people, there are those who seek to poison the holy source of the Republic's strength with vice. That is the most devious, dangerous and abominable attack on liberty. The libertine is an enemy of the state, the more he seems to serve liberty, the greater the danger. The most dangerous citizen is he who wears out a dozen fashionable red caps without doing one single revolutionary deed.

Whom do I mean? Just think of those who once lived in attics and now drive in carriages and fornicate with marchionesses and baronesses. We may well ask, where did this wealth come from? Did they rob the people or shake the gold hands of foreign kings? You see them! These 'tribunes of the people' parading the vice and luxury of the old court, these marquises and counts of the Revolution marrying rich wives, giving lavish banquets, gambling, being waited upon by servants, wearing sumptuous clothes. Why am I suddenly reminded of the enemies of the Roman Republic, why at this dangerous moment could I speak of the Catiline Conspiracy? But no, the portraits are complete.

No truce, no peace with the men who robbed the people and go unpunished, for whom the Republic was a financial swindle and the Revolution a business. Terrified, they are trying to douse the Revolution's fire. I hear them say to themselves 'We must be free to speak our minds, be true to our natures, which are full of vice, we are not virtuous enough to be so terrible. Oh lawmakers, pity our weakness, do not be cruel with your terror.'

Be calm you virtuous people, be calm patriots, tell your brothers in Lyons how the sword of justice does not sleep in the hands to which you entrusted it. We will give the Republic a great example.

General applause.

Many Voices   Long live the Republic, long live Robespierre!

Scene Four

A corridor in the Jacobin Club.

Lacroix, Legendre.

Lacroix   What have you done, Legendre? Do you know whose head you've knocked off, with your 'statues'?

Legendre   A few dandies, a few fancy women, that's all.

Lacroix   You're a suicide. A shadow that murders the body that casts it.

Legendre   What do you mean?

Lacroix   Collot was clear enough.

Legendre   So what?

Lacroix   Don't you see? You've made the counter-revolution official and public. Now Robespierre and Saint-Just will have to act, you've forced their hand!

Legendre   Where's Danton?

Lacroix   How do I know? Trying to put the Venus de Milo back together bit by bit, from all the tarts in the Palais

Royal. Working on his mosaic, he calls it. I wonder what limb he's on now? Let's go and find him.

They go.

Scene Five

A room in the Palais Royale.

Danton, Marion.

Marion No, leave me alone, at your feet, like this. I want to tell you a story.

Danton You could use your lips for something better.

Marion No, leave me be. My mother was a good woman. When she gave me a book to read, there were always pages torn out. She didn't pull pages out of the Bible though. But there were things in the Bible I didn't understand. I didn't dare ask anyone, so I brooded on them, alone.

I began to grow up, my body changed. Spring came. All around me I felt something going on I had no part in. I was lost in my own world, a mood came over me, a strange feeling, there was a weird atmosphere around me, it almost choked me.

Then my mother invited a young man to the house. He was good-looking. He said extraordinary things. I didn't understand but he made me laugh. My mother invited him a lot. And if pleasure is yours for the taking, why not take it? So we did, again and again, on the sly. It was lovely. But I began to have other men. All the men's bodies merged into one, I became like an ocean, swallowing everything up, getting deeper and deeper. That's how I'm made, can we help how we're made?

Then he found out. One morning he kissed me then held his hands tight about my neck, choking me. Then he laughed. He said he didn't want to spoil my fun. That my body was all the finery I had, I'd need it, it would be torn and dirty and worn out sooner than I knew. He left. That evening I was sitting at a window, staring at the sunset. To me the world is vague, I don't think, just feel. I was lost in the waves of golden light. Then a crowd came down the street with children dancing in front of it. Women were looking out of the windows. They were carrying him past in a big basket. The light shone on his pale face, his curls were damp. He'd drowned himself. I wept with a terrible longing. My life has no beginnings, no endings. All I know is an endless longing and grasping, an endless fire, an endless river. My mother died of grief because of me, people point their fingers at me.

They're stupid. It all comes down to one thing: what gives you pleasure? It can be bodies, pictures of Jesus, flowers, children's toys. It's all the same feeling. Pleasure is the best kind of prayer.

Danton   Why can't I quite take in all of your beauty, embrace it all at once?

Marion   Danton, your lips have eyes.

Danton   I'd like to be part of the air, I'd bathe you in a flood of me, break against every wave of your body.

Enter **Lacroix** *and* **Legendre**.

Lacroix   Danton, listen. We were at the Jacobins.

Danton   Ah. And what news?

Lacroix   The representatives from Lyons read a proclamation. The gist of it: they despair and pull their togas about them, their daggers are drawn and they are ready for suicide. Legendre shouted out that reactionaries want to tear down the statues of Chalier and Marat. The terror is making him lose his mind. Children tug his coat in the street, playing at pulling him to the guillotine. He tries to be safe by pretending to be a revolutionary monster.

Danton   And Robespierre?

Lacroix   Drummed his fingers on the podium and said 'Virtue must live by terror'. I felt a twinge in my neck hearing that.

Danton   They plane planks for the guillotine.

Lacroix   And Collot shouted like a madman 'tear off the masks'.

Danton   Do that and the faces will come off with them.

Hérault-Séchelles *enters.*

What's happening, Hérault?

Hérault   I went straight from the Jacobins to Robespierre. I demanded an explanation. He tried to put on the look of Brutus, killing his sons. He ranted a lot of stuff about 'duty', said when it came to liberty he was ruthless, he'd sacrifice everything, himself, brothers, friends.

Danton   Well that's clear. One twist in the situation and he'll be holding the basket for his nearest and dearest. We should thank Legendre for making him speak out.

Lacroix   I don't know. The deprivation amongst the people is overwhelming. Their suffering is a terrible lever. Robespierre must find more enemies to blame.

Danton   The Revolution is like Saturn, it eats its own children. *(After some thought.)* No! They won't dare.

Lacroix   Danton, you're a saint of the people. But a dead saint and the Revolution doesn't deal in relics, it's thrown the bones of kings into the street and smashed all the images and statues in the churches. Do you think they'll let you be some kind of monument?

Danton   My name! The people!

Lacroix   Your name? You're a moderate! So am I, so is Camille, Hérault, Philippeau. To the people moderation and weakness are the same thing. They kill all stragglers.

I tell you: the timid tailors, who tremble sewing red bonnets for the crowds at the executions? Even they would feel the full force of Roman history in their needles if they got it into their heads that the man who led the September massacres is, actually, a moderate!

Danton   True, true. And the people are like children, they smash everything to see what's inside.

Lacroix   And Danton, we are what Robespierre says we are: vice-ridden libertines. We enjoy life. But the people are virtuous, they don't enjoy life at all, how can they, work dulls them, their senses are clogged up with dullness. They don't drink because they're broke, they don't go to brothels because their breath stinks of cheese and pickled herrings and disgusts the girls.

Danton   They hate people who enjoy life like a eunuch hates men.

Lacroix   We get called scoundrels and (*leaning into* **Danton**'s *ear*) between ourselves there's more than a little truth there. Robespierre and the people *are* virtuous. Saint-Just will write a philosophical treatise on it and Barère, Barère will tailor a speech to clothe the Convention in blood and . . . I see it all.

Danton   You're dreaming! They'll never have courage without me. The Revolution isn't over yet, they'll need me again, they'll keep me in their arsenal.

Lacroix   But we must act. Now.

Danton   It'll sort itself out.

Lacroix   Sort itself out with us dead.

Marion (*to* **Danton**)   Your lips have gone cold. Words have stifled your kisses.

Danton   Yes, so many kisses lost to words. Thank you, high politics, for interrupting our lowly pleasures. (*To* **Lacroix**.) I'll go and see Robespierre later. I'll provoke him, jab at him, he won't be able to hold in what he's really up to.

But first, give me a little time. Goodnight my friends, goodnight, I thank you.

Lacroix   Goodnight Danton. Be careful: that girl's thighs will guillotine you. Come on then, friends.

Scene Six

Tuileries Palace. Offices of the Committee of Public Safety.

Robespierre, Danton, Hérault.

Robespierre   I tell you, he who pulls back my arm when I draw my sword is my enemy. His motives are irrelevant. Anyone who stops me defending myself kills me as surely as if he attacked me.

Danton   Where self-defence ends, murder begins. I see no reason that compels us to go on killing.

Robespierre   The social revolution isn't over yet. He who makes only half a revolution digs his own grave. The old ruling class is not yet dead. The healthy vigour of the people must completely take the place of that class, which is worn out and decadent. Vice must be punished, virtue must rule through terror.

Danton   I don't understand the word 'punishment'. You and your virtue, Robespierre! You take no bribes, run up no debts, sleep with no women, always wear a clean coat and never get drunk. Robespierre, you are abominably virtuous. I'd be disgusted with myself if I'd spent thirty years with such a self-righteous expression stuck on my face, running about between heaven and earth, only for the miserable pleasure of finding people worse than myself. Is there nothing in you, not just a little bit of you, that very occasionally, very quietly, whispers: 'you lie! You lie!'

Robespierre   My conscience is clear.

Danton   Conscience is a mirror for apes to look in and torment themselves. We all dress ourselves up in high morals, then go out on the town to have our fun. Why get all hot and bothered about it? I say: to each of us our own pleasure, and the right to defend ourselves against anyone who tries to stop it.

Robespierre Do you deny virtue?

Danton And vice. There are only Epicureans, some are fine, some are gross. Christ was the finest of all. That's the only difference I can see between people. We act according to our natures, that is: we do what makes us feel good. Eh, Incorruptible! A shock is it, to have the crutch you call virtue kicked away from you? Eh, Maxime?

Robespierre Georges, at certain times vice is high treason.

Danton Oh no, don't ban it, that would be ungrateful, you are deeply in its debt. Purity needs vice, if only for the contrast. To use your terminology: our blows must serve the Republic. We can't strike down the innocent and the guilty at the same time.

Robespierre Who said one innocent person has been struck down?

Danton You hear that, Hérault? No one innocent has died. (*He goes off, addressing* **Hérault** *as he leaves.*) We must move, now! We must declare ourselves!

Danton *and* **Hérault** *go off.*

Robespierre (*alone*) Go then. He wants the fiery steeds of the Revolution to stop at the nearest brothel, as if he was a coachman with a team of nags. But they'll bolt and drag him to the Place de la Révolution.

Kick my high heels? Use my terminology? Mine?

No, stop. Is that what they'll say? That his gigantic bulk cast a shadow over me and that is why I sent him out of the sun? For personal spite?

Would they be right?

Is it really necessary? Yes! Yes! The Republic! He must go.

My thoughts watch each other. He must go. He who stands
still in a crowd that presses forward, in effect moves
backwards against it and will be trampled underfoot.

No virtue? Virtue my crutch? My terminology? Thought
against thought, why can't I stop?

A pause.

There. There. Something inside me, telling lies to all the
rest of me.

He goes to the window.

Night snores over the earth and shifts in a desolate dream.
Insubstantial thoughts, desires barely guessed at, confused,
formless, which can't live in the daylight, now take shape
and sneak into the house of dreams. They open the doors,
stare out of the windows, they become half-flesh, the limbs
stretch, the lips move. And when we wake everything might
seem brighter, but aren't we still in a dream? Oh what the
mind does, who can blame us? The mind goes through
more actions in one hour than the lumbering body does in a
year. A thought may be a sin, but whether or not that
thought becomes a deed, whether the body acts on it, is
chance. Just chance.

Saint-Just *comes on.*

Who's there in the dark? Light! Light!

Saint-Just   Don't you know my voice?

Robespierre   Ah. You, Saint-Just.

*A **Servant Girl** brings a light.*

Saint-Just   Were you alone?

Robespierre   Danton just left.

Saint-Just   I saw him earlier, in the Palais Royal. He was
wearing his revolutionary face and spouting epigrams. He
was on Christian names with the sans-culottes, the tarts

were yapping at his heels, the crowd hung about whispering every word he said. We're losing the advantage. Why do you hesitate? If we must we'll act without you. We're resolved.

Robespierre   What do you want to do?

Saint-Just   Call the Committees, Legislative, General Security and Public Safety, to a special session.

Robepierre   A grand affair.

Saint-Just   We must bury the great corpse with dignity, like priests, not assassins. We can't hack it up piece by piece, torso head limbs must go down whole.

Robepierre   Be plain.

Saint-Just   We must lay him to rest in full armour. Slaughter his horses and his slaves on his burial mound. Lacroix –

Robespierre   An outright criminal. A lawyer's clerk, now Lieutenant-General of France. Go on.

Saint-Just   Hérault-Séchelles.

Robespierre   A handsome head.

Saint-Just   He may have penned the first letter of the Constitution beautifully. But we no longer need ornamental flourishes. He will be effaced. Camille Desmoulins . . .

Robespierre   Camille?

Saint-Just (*handing him a paper*)   I thought that would startle you. Read that.

Robespierre   'Le Vieux Cordelier'? That's nothing. Childish satire. Camille's making fun of you.

Saint-Just   Read here, here. (*He points at a place.*)

Robespierre   'This Messiah of blood, Robespierre, this Christ in reverse, stands on his Calvary. He is not sacrificed, he sacrifices. The devout sisters of the guillotine stand below like Mary and Magdalene. Saint-Just, like St John the Evangelist, delivers the apocalyptic revelations of the Master to the Convention; he holds up his head with a holy look, as if it were the sacrament itself.'

Saint-Just   I'll make him hold his under his arm.

Robespierre (*reads on*)   'The clean frock coat of the Messiah is France's winding sheet; his fingers rapping on the podium of the tribunal are the blades of the guillotine. And you, Barère, who said that coins not heads were being struck in the Place de la Révolution – but I won't upset that old hag. Yes I will. Why is he an old hag? Because he is like a widow who has driven half a dozen husbands to their graves. It's a talent: people he smiles upon have a habit of dying six months later. What can one do for a man who sits by the corpses of his friends to enjoy the stink?'

Oh Camille, you too?

Down with them! Now! Only the dead are harmless. Have you drafted the indictments?

Saint-Just   I can easily. You said it all at the Jacobin Club.

Robespierre   I wanted to frighten them.

Saint-Just   I'll elaborate a little. Start with an hors-d'oeuvre of swindlers, end with a dessert of foreign spies. A meal they'll choke to death on, I promise.

Robespierre   Do it quickly! No long death agony! These past few days I've become . . . sensitive. Just be quick!

Saint-Just *goes off.*

Messiah of blood, who is not sacrificed but sacrifices. The Son of Man is crucified in all of us, we all agonise in a bloody sweat, each in our own Gethsemane. But no one redeems anyone else with their wounds. Oh my Camille! They all go from me. The night is bleak and empty. I'm alone.

Act Two

Scene One

A room in **Danton**'s *house. Night.*

Danton (*at the window*)   Will it never stop? Will the light never die, the noise stop? Will it never be dark and silent to spare us the sight and sound of our foul sins? September! September! September!

Julie (*calling from another room*)   Danton! Danton!

Danton   Eh?

Julie (*enters*)   You were shouting.

Danton   Was I?

Julie   You shouted 'foul sins'. Then 'September'.

Danton   Me? No, didn't say a thing. They were just faint, secret thoughts.

Julie   You're trembling.

Danton   Trembling? What do you expect when the walls begin to speak, when your body breaks apart and thoughts stagger around speaking from bricks and stones? It's not good.

Julie   Georges, my Georges . . .

Danton   Stop thinking altogether if thought's going to turn straight into speech. There are some thoughts that must never, ever be heard. Not good if they cry out the second they're born, like a baby from the room. Not good.

Julie   God keep your reason, Georges. Georges do you know who I am?

Danton   A human being, a woman, my wife Julie. And the world has five continents: Europe, Asia, Africa, America,

Australia, and two and two are four. Yes, reason still there. I shouted September?

Julie   Yes, Danton, I heard it through the whole house.

Danton   I went to the window and . . . (*He looks out.*) The city's quiet, the lights are out . . .

Julie   There's a child crying somewhere.

Danton   I went to the window and . . . there was a cry of outrage, echoing through all the streets and alleys: September!

Julie   You were dreaming, Danton. Come . . .

Danton   Dreaming. But there was something else. My head's swimming, wait. There! I remember. The earth's globe was panting, as it span in space. My limbs were gigantic, I pounced on the globe and rode it bareback like a runaway horse, I gripped its flanks with my thighs, I clutched its mane, my hair streamed above the abyss, I shouted in terror . . . and woke. Then I got up, went to the window and heard that word, Julie. Why that word? What does that word want of me, why does it reach out its bloody hands?

My brain's numb, Julie, September . . .

Julie   The armies of the foreign kings were forty hours from Paris . . .

Danton   Our border's defences had been smashed, the fortresses of Longwy and Verdun had fallen, aristocrats were loose in the city . . .

Julie   The Republic was lost.

Danton   Lost. We couldn't leave the enemy at our backs, we'd have been fools. Two enemies on a plank. Them or us. The stronger knocks the weaker off. Fair? Fair, no?

Julie   Yes, yes.

Danton   It wasn't murder, it was civil war.

Julie   You saved your country.

Danton   I did, I did. We had to do it, it was self-defence.
The man on the cross took the easy way out: 'It must needs
be that offences come, but woe to that man by whom the
offence cometh.' 'Needs be.' It was necessary. Who can curse
the hand on which the curse of necessity falls? What is it in
us that whores, lies, steals, murders?

Julie   Oh Georges Danton, you are a leader, whether you
want to be or not. All the rest is . . . night fears.

Danton   Night fears. I feel calmer now.

Julie   Quite calm, my love.

Danton   Yes, Julie. Come to bed.

Scene Two

Danton's *house*.

Danton, Lacroix, Hérault, Camille Desmoulins, Legendre.

Camille   Quick, Danton. We're losing time.

Danton (*getting dressed*)   No, time's losing us. You pull on
your shirt, you pull your trousers up over it, you crawl into
bed at night and out in the morning, you put one foot in
front of the other. Sad. There's absolutely no vision of
another way of doing it, millions have always done it like
that, millions always will. And since we're split into two
halves, two arms and two legs, everything must be done
twice. It's very, very sad.

Camille   You're talking childishly.

Danton   Dying men are often childish.

Lacroix   By delaying you rush headlong towards ruin,
and you're dragging your friends down with you. Rally the
cowards, from all the parties. Cry out against the tyranny of

the Committee of Public Safety. Speak of daggers, Brutus, frighten Robespierre's cronies, use anyone, even what remains of the Leftists. Give rip to your anger! Don't let us die humiliated and helpless, like the wretched Hébert.

Danton   But don't you remember you called me a dead saint? You were horribly near the truth. I went to talk to some people on the ground, in the sections. They were respectful but like mourners at a funeral. You were right, I'm a relic and relics get thrown out in the street.

Lacroix   Why did you let it come to this?

Danton   Come to this? I got bored. Bored, going round wearing the same coat, pulling the same face. Contemptible. A pathetic instrument with one string, one note, I just couldn't go on, I wanted a rest. Well, I've got it. The Revolution's offering me retirement, though in a rather different way than I thought. Besides, who supports me? Our whores might confront the nuns of the guillotine, but who else will? And count up who's against us: the Jacobin Club has declared virtue the order of the day, the Cordelier club calls me Hébert's executioner and the Convention . . . well, we could try to win there, but it would be a long, messy struggle. Robespierre is the dogma of the Revolution, it can't be denied. No, it won't work. We didn't make the Revolution, the Revolution made us. And even if it did work I'd rather be guillotined than guillotine. I no longer understand why we still fight each other, we should sit down and have peace. We were botched when we were created, we lack something, some element. I can't name it, but we won't find it by pulling out each other's guts and scrabbling around in our entrails. Bah, we are pitiful alchemists.

Camille   Translated into the grand, tragic style, that would go like this: how long must mankind eat its own limbs in eternal hunger? Or: how must humanity, marooned on a wreck, suck each other's blood in unquenchable thirst? Or: how long must we algebraists of the flesh, hunting for the ever elusive and unknown 'x' write out equations in mangled limbs?

Danton   My echo.

Camille   Aren't I. You fire the pistol, I come back with a crash of thunder. That's why you should keep me at your side.

Hérault   So France is left with her executioners?

Danton   People are fine. They're oppressed, but at least they're not bored. They can be noble, fine-feeling, virtuous, witty, what more do they want? What's it matter if you die by guillotine, or by fever or old age? Better to be young and supple, as you stride from the stage saying your last lines on earth. The audience applauds and we all love it! It's all gesture, all acting, even if you do get really stabbed to death at the end. Excellent thing, to shorten life a little. And, above all: I'd have to shout. It's too much effort. Life isn't worth all the sweat and strain needed, merely to hang on to it.

Hérault   Then run, Danton, get away!

Danton   Can you take your country with you on the soles of your shoes? And anyway, when it comes down to it: they won't dare. (*To* **Camille**.) Come on, my boy. I tell you, they will not dare! So, adieu! Adieu!

Hérault   What do we do now?

Lacroix   Go home, like Lucrece, and prepare to die gracefully.

Scene Three

Tuileries Palace. Offices of the Committee of Public Safety.

Robespierre, Saint-Just.

Robespierre   Is that the document?

Saint-Just   You mean the warrant for Danton's arrest? Oh yes.

Robespierre   Signed by the Committee?

Saint-Just   All of us. But for you.

Robespierre   Give it here. (*He takes the document.*) Is it legally in order?

Saint-Just   If we say it is.

Robespierre   The formalities must be observed.

Saint-Just   Oh, blood will flow in exquisitely formal patterns.

Robespierre (*he finishes reading*)   Maybe there are enough names signed on this already.

Saint-Just   Maxime, only one name is really needed there.

Robespierre   Yes, it is always me. You all hide behind me. I am seen as the monster, you just as my shadows.

Robespierre *signs quickly.*

Saint-Just   Writ very small.

Robespierre   Large enough.

Scene Four

The Palais Royale.

Danton, Camille, Hérault, Lucile.

Hérault   You must see that new play: the hanging gardens of Babylon! A maze of vaults, stairways, corridors, flung up into the air with extraordinary ease.

Camille   It will fail. All they want in their theatres is crudely carved puppets with the strings moving it up and down and legs creaking along in blank verse, and they say 'What truth! What understanding of human nature, how profound!' But turn them out into the street and, oh dear, reality is too sordid. Creation is being newly born every minute, within them and all around them, glowing, a storm glittering with lightning; but they see and hear nothing. They go to the theatre, read poems and novels and praise the caricatures. To Creation itself they say: 'How ugly, how boring.'

Danton But artists treat nature like David. In the September massacres, when the corpses of murdered prisoners were thrown out onto the street, he stood there cold-bloodedly sketching them. He said: 'I'm catching the last twitches of life in these bastards.'

Danton *is called outside*.

Camille What do you say, Lucile?

Lucile Nothing.

Camille But do you listen?

Lucile Of course!

Camille So am I right? Do you really hear what I say?

Lucile Actually, no. Not really.

Danton *returns*.

Camille What's wrong?

Danton The Committee of Public Safety has decided to arrest me. Someone's warned me and offered me a place to hide. They want my head? Let them have it. I'm sick of this rigmarole. What's it matter? I'll know how to die with courage, it's easier than living.

Camille Danton, there's still time . . .

Danton No no. But I never thought they'd . . .

Camille Danton, your laziness!

Danton I'm not lazy, just tired. I ache all over, the soles of my feet are burning.

Camille　Where are you going?

Danton　If only I knew

Camille　No seriously, where?

Danton　I'm going for a walk, my boy, a walk.

Danton *goes off.*

Hérault　I'll go to the Tuileries, get more news.

Camille　Yes.

Hérault *goes off.*

Lucile　Camille!

Camille　No no, calm down.

Lucile　But when I think . . . this head, they . . . Camille, it's all madness isn't it?

Camille　Don't worry, I'm no Danton.

Lucile　The world's such a big place, so full of things. Full of other men's heads . . . so who's got the right to take this one away from me, what use is it to them? It's evil.

Camille　I said calm down, there's no need to worry. I spoke to Robespierre, yesterday. He was very friendly. It's true things have been tense between us lately but we have different ways of looking at things, that's all.

Lucile　Go and see him.

Camille　We sat at the same desk at school. He was always moody and lonely. I was the only one who made a point of talking to him. I even made him laugh sometimes. He's always been very fond of me. Right, I'm off.

Lucile　Now? All right go. No, come here, this . . . (*She kisses him.*) and this! Go! Go!

Camille *goes off.*

(Sings.)

> Oh leaving, leaving you my friend
> Who thought that love would end?

That song suddenly in my head, why? No, that's not good, not good at all. Just then, when he turned away, I thought: I'll never see him turn back, or look at me again, he'll just go further and further away . . . this room's so empty. The windows are all open, like they've laid out a corpse in here. I can't bear it.

She goes off.

Scene Five

Open country.

Danton I won't go on, disturbing the silence, feet scuffing, lungs panting.

He sits down. A pause.

Someone told me, once, there's a disease that makes you lose your memory. Death must be like that. I hope he'll do more and wipe out everything. I hope he will. My memories are my enemies. I'd turn my cheek, like a good Christian, and offer them salvation gladly. It's safe here in the country? Hunh. Safe for memories, but not for me. My only safety is in the grave. There memory will be obliterated, I'll be able to *forget*. But away from Paris, here, my memory lives. Which is it to be, me or it? The answer's simple.

He stands and turns back.

I'm flirting with death! It's rather fun, ogling him from a distance through my lorgnette. This business makes me laugh. A sense of permanence tells me there'll be a tomorrow after today, a day after tomorrow, everything as it is now. Empty threats! They only want to frighten me. They will not dare.

Scene Six

The National Convention. **Deputies** *huddle with* **Legendre**.

Legendre   Is the butchery of deputies to go on? Now they have arrested Danton, who is safe? If he falls we all go down.

1ˢᵗ Deputy   What can we do?

2ⁿᵈ Deputy   He must be tried by the Convention. Success will be ours. Nothing can drown that voice.

3ʳᵈ Deputy   Impossible. A decree prevents that.

Legendre   Repeal it. Make an exception. I'll put the motion. I rely on your support.

Legendre *makes his way to the podium.*

1ˢᵗ Deputy   Is he the right man to do this?

2ⁿᵈ Deputy   You think he's not up to it?

1ˢᵗ Deputy   I don't know. The mood is ugly.

1ˢᵗ Deputy   See what he says.

President   The session is open.

Legendre (*ascends the tribunal*)   Last night four members of the National Convention were arrested. Danton is one of them. The names of the others I do not know. But I demand they be tried before the Assembly. Citizens! I hold Danton to be as spotless as myself and I reproach myself with nothing. I attack no members of the Committee of Public Safety or General Security, but I fear there are personal feuds, private hatreds that may rob Liberty of men who gave her great service. The man who by his energy, his passion saved France in 1792 deserves a hearing. If he, indeed, is to stand accused of high treason, give him the right to defend himself.

Violent commotion.

A Few Voices   We support Legendre's motion.

1ˢᵗ Deputy   The people put us here. Only they can get rid of us.

2ⁿᵈ Deputy   Your words stink of corpses. Words out of the mouths of aristos! No privileges! The axe of justice is raised over every head!

3ʳᵈ Deputy   Our Committees must not withhold the sanctuary of the law from our legislators and send them to the guillotine!

4ᵗʰ Deputy   Crime has no sanctuary! Only criminals in crowns find sanctuary, on their thrones.

5ᵗʰ Deputy   Only criminals ask for sanctuary.

6ᵗʰ Deputy   Only assassins deny it.

Robespierre   Not for many a long day has this assembly been thrown into such confusion. And no wonder: we have come to a crisis. Today will decide whether a handful of men will, or will not, defeat their country. How can you betray your principles so far that, today, you will grant to a few individuals what yesterday you denied Chabot, Delaunay and Fabre? What is behind this favouritism to a few men? What do I care about the hymns of praise people sing about themselves and their friends? We know their true worth. We do not ask if a man did this or that patriotic act, we question his entire political career. Legendre appears to be ignorant of the names of the detainees. But the whole Convention knows them. Who is amongst them? His friend Lacroix. He names Danton because he thinks a special privilege is attached to that name. We want no privileges, we want no false gods!

Applause.

What sets Danton above Lafayette or Dumouriez, Brissot, Fabre, Chabot, Hébert? What did we say about them that we cannot say about him? Did you spare them? What has he done to deserve privileges above his fellow citizens? Could it be that a few deluded men, and others less deluded, lined up behind him in the hope of a free ride to success and power? The greater, then, his betrayal of true patriots who put their trust in him, the more severely must he feel the wrath of lovers of liberty.

They are trying to fill you with fear of abuse of power. The power that you yourselves wield. They cry out against the tyranny of the Committees. But you bring the trust of the people to the Committees, that trust is an absolute protection for true patriots. Anyone would think we are all trembling in fear. But I tell you, he who trembles at this moment is guilty, for innocence never trembles before public vigilance.

General applause.

They tried to scare me too. They wrote to me. They warned me that I am surrounded by Danton's friends, that the danger he faces could, in turn, come to me. With these threats, cloaked in false virtues and appeals to old loyalties, they tried to moderate my zeal and passion for liberty. So I now declare: nothing will stand in my way, not even if Danton's danger becomes my own. All of us need a degree of courage and greatness of spirit. Only criminals and the spiritually crippled are afraid to see their kind fall by their side. For, when they are no longer hidden in a crowd of accomplices, they find themselves naked and exposed in the harsh light of truth. But if there are spiritual cripples in this assembly, there are also heroes. The number of criminals is not that great. We need only strike off a few heads and the country will be saved.

Applause.

I demand that Legendre's motion be rejected.

*The **Deputies** rise as a body to indicate their unanimous agreement.*

Saint-Just It seems that there are, in this assembly, a few
sensitive ears that cannot stand the word 'blood'. A few
general observations will show them that we are no more
cruel than nature or the age we live in. Nature obeys her
laws calmly and inexorably. If man comes into conflict with
them he is destroyed. A change in the constituent parts of
the air, a flare-up of subterranean fires, a fluctuation in the
water level, a plague, a volcanic eruption, a flood, these
send thousands to their graves. But what is the final
reckoning? An insignificant, almost imperceptible change in
physical nature, which would almost leave no trace, but for
the corpses which lie in its wake.

So I ask you now: should moral nature, as it goes about its
revolutions, be more cautious than physical nature? Should
not an idea, just like a law of physics, be allowed to destroy
what opposes it? Why should an event that transforms the
whole of humanity not advance through blood? The world
spirit employs the sword in the moral sphere, just as he
employs volcanoes or floods in the physical. What is the
difference between death by plague and death by
revolution?

Mankind advances slowly. Its steps can only be counted
centuries later. Behind each footprint rise the graves of
generations. The achievements of the simplest inventions
and principles cost the lives of millions. Is it not to be
expected that now, when history speeds faster that ever
before, many men will fall, their last breath spent?

The conclusion is simple. We were all created in the same
way. But for the minor variations made by nature herself,
we are all equal. Therefore, everyone is superior and no
one is privileged, neither an individual or a smaller or
larger class of individuals. And every clause of that sentence,
when put into practice, has killed people! The 14th of July,
10th of August and the 31st of May are its punctuation
marks. The physical world would take centuries to do what
we have done, punctuated by generations. We took four

years. Is it, then, so surprising that at every turn of the tide the great sea of the Revolution washes up its corpses?

We still have a few clauses to complete our sentence. Are a few more corpses going to stop us? Moses led his people across the Red Sea and the desert and let the old, corrupt generation die out before he founded his new state. We do not have the Red Sea or the desert, we have war and the guillotine.

The Revolution cuts up mankind to rejuvenate it. Humanity will emerge from the bloodbath like the world after the flood, restored, newly created.

Long drawn out applause. Some **Deputies** *leap to their feet in their enthusiasm.*

All you secret enemies of tyranny, in Europe, in the whole world, who carry Brutus's dagger under your robes, come! Join us at this sublime moment.

The **Deputies** *and* **Others** *strike up the 'Marseillaise'.*

Act Three

Scene One

The Luxembourg Palace. A room containing **Prisoners**. **Hérault de Séchelles** *is amongst them, also the haggard figure of* **General Dillon**. **Danton, Lacroix** *and* **Camille** *are led in.*

Hérault (*rushes to* **Danton** *and embraces him*)   Do I say good morning or good night? I won't ask if you've slept. Or if we'll ever sleep again.

Danton   Oh we will, by going to bed laughing.

Dillon   A bull mastiff dog with the wings of a dove. The evil genius of the Revolution. He tried to rape his own mother but she was too strong for him.

1st Prisoner   His life and his death are equal calamities.

Lacroix (*to* **Danton**)   I didn't think they'd arrest us so quickly.

Danton   I did.

Lacroix   And you said nothing?

Danton   I . . . didn't think they'd dare. (*To* **Hérault**.) Better to be under the earth than giving yourself corns running around on top of it, eh? I prefer the earth as a pillow rather than a hassock.

Hérault   At least we won't have old men's leathery skin on our fingers, when we stroke the cheeks of the lovely lady putrefaction.

Camille (*to* **Danton**)   I fear you've left it too late, Danton. No matter how far you stick your tongue out now you'll not lick the sweat of death off your forehead. Oh Lucile, what a tragedy.

The **Prisoners** *gather round the new arrivals.*

Dillon (*to* **Danton**)   You spilt the blood of my friends, now it has drowned you.

1st Prisoner (*to* **Hérault**)   Yes Hérault, what was it you said at the trial of the Girondins? 'The power of the people and the power of reason are one and the same.'

2nd Prisoner (*to* **Camille**)   Hey, inspector of lanterns. Have the corpses hung in the street given France enlightenment?

3rd Prisoner   Let him alone. Those lips said the word 'mercy'.

He embraces **Camille**. *Other* **Prisoners** *follow his example.*

Hérault   Mercy? Oh yes. We're priests who prayed for the dying and caught their disease.

Several Voices   The blow that strikes you, kills all of us.

Camille   Gentlemen, I apologise. We tried to stop the killing, but couldn't. Now I go to the scaffold because my eyes watered at the fate of a few unhappy men.

Lacroix (*to one of the* **Prisoners**)   How can there be so many in these wretched circumstances?

3rd Prisoner   Didn't the tumbrils tell you? Paris is a butcher's block.

Dillon   You know all about it, Lacroix. Equality swings her sickle over all our heads, the lava of the Revolution flows, the guillotine makes Republicans of us all.

Danton (*to* **Lacroix**)   Who is that man?

Lacrox   General Dillon.

Danton   Dillon? So changed.

Lacroix   When we executed his fellow Girondins he went into hiding. The Watch arrested him, drunk in a cellar.

Danton (*laughs*)   And now we're cell mates. History has a way of biting you in the arse, eh Lacroix?

Dillon   Danton, you and your cronies, look around you, you spoke this! Follow the logic of your fine phrases, see them become flesh and blood. This is your rhetoric, translated. These wretches, these executioners, the guillotine are your speeches come to life. You have built your doctrines out of human heads.

Danton You're right, General. Today everything is worked in human flesh. That is the curse of our age. Now my body is to be a building block. It's a year since I founded the Revolutionary Tribunal. I ask pardon for that, from God and man. I want to prevent new September massacres, to save the innocent. But this slow murder, with its grotesque formalities, is more horrible than what went before. Gentlemen, I hoped to free you.

Mercier Oh, we'll be free all right.

Danton Now I find . . . I myself sharing your predicament. And I don't know how it will end.

Scene Two

A room. **Collot d'Herbois, Herman**.

Collot Everything ready?

Herman It's going to be hard. If Danton weren't among them, there'd be no problem.

Collot He must lead the dance.

Herman He'll frighten the jury. He's the Revolution's scarecrow.

Collot The jury must say 'Guilty'.

Herman There is a way. It's a little contemptuous of legal procedure.

Collot Out with it.

Herman We don't draw lots for the jury, we handpick our men.

Collot That should work. It'll be a good bonfire. I've thrown in a few more accused: four forgers, a couple of pimps, a few bankers. A tasty dish, just what the people need. Right, reliable jurors, who?

Herman Leroi, he's deaf. He never hears anything the defendants say. Danton can shout himself hoarse there.

Collot Who else?

Herman Vilatte, our resident alcoholic and Lumière who sleeps all the time. Just kick them and they'll yell 'Guilty!'. Then Girard, who works on the principle that anyone who appears before the Tribunal is automatically condemned. Then Renaudin . . .

Collot Him? He once helped priests to escape.

Herman Don't worry. He came to see me a few days ago. He demanded that all condemned men be bled from the veins to tone them down a bit, he doesn't like their defiant attitude.

Collot Excellent. You know who depends on you.

Herman Just leave it to me.

Scene Three

The Revolutionary Tribunal.

Herman (*to* **Danton**) Your name, citizen?

Danton The Revolution proclaims my name, it is in the pantheon of history. As for my place of residence, that will soon be the void.

Herman Danton. The Convention accuses you of having conspired with Mirabeau, with Dumouriez, with the Duke of Orléans, with the Girondins, the foreigners and the aristocratic faction of Louis XVII.

Danton   My voice, which rang out so often in the people's cause, will refute these slanders. Let the scum who accuse me come here and I will heap shame upon them. Call the Committees to the Tribunal. I will answer only before them. They are my prosecutors and my witnesses. Call them! Make them show themselves! Besides, what do you and your verdict matter to me? I've told you. The void will soon be my sanctuary. Life is a burden, take it from me, I will be glad.

Herman   Danton. Bravado is the mark of guilt, composure a sign of innocence.

Danton   Bravado is, no doubt, a fault. But that national bravado, the bravado of defiance with which I fought for liberty, that is the greatest of all virtues. I invoke that sense of daring, that defiance now, in the name of the Republic and against my accusers. What composure can there be from me when I find myself slandered so basely? I am a revolutionary. You can't expect a cool and modest defence from my kind. Men of my stamp are beyond price to the Revolution, the genius of liberty shines from our brows.

Signs of applause among the listeners.

I am accused of conspiring with Mirabeau, with Dumouriez, with Orléans, of crawling at the feet of wretched despots. I am summoned to answer before (*quoting from the indictment before him*) 'inexorable and unswerving justice'. I, I am!

Saint-Just, you miserable man, you will answer to posterity for this slander!

Herman   I demand you answer calmly. Remember, Marat showed respect to his judges.

Danton   They have laid hands on my whole life. Let it stand up, let it fight back! I will bury them beneath the weight of all my deeds.

I am not arrogant about what I have done. Fate guides everyone's arm. But only a mighty personality can be fate's instrument.

On the Champs de Mars I declared war on the monarchy, on the 10th of August I attacked it, on the 21st of January I killed it and threw down a king's head, a gauntlet to all monarchs.

Repeated signs of applause. He picks up the indictment.

I glance at this scandalous tissue of lies. My whole being is shaken. Who are they, who had to force Danton into the Champs de Mars? Who are these wondrous beings from whom he had to steal his strength? Let my accusers appear! I know what I do by making that demand. I will tear the masks from these villains and hurl them back into the darkness, from which they should never have crawled.

Herman (*rings a bell*)   Don't you hear the bell?

Danton   The voice of a man, defending his honour and his life, drowns your bell!

In September I fed the young brood of the Revolution with morsels of aristocrat flesh. My voice forged weapons for the people from the gold of the rich and the aristocracy. My voice was the hurricane that drowned the lackeys of the despots under waves of bayonets.

Loud applause.

Herman   Danton, your voice is cracked. You're over-wrought. Conclude your defence later. You need rest. The session is closed.

Danton   Now you see me! A few more hours and Danton will die in the arms of glory!

Scene Four

Julie *with newspapers. A* **Servant** *waits.*

Julie (*reading, skimming*)   Danton is frightening the tribunal
. . . The jury is divided, the assembly is unhappy . . .
Extraordinary crowds: thousands took to the streets during
the day's hearing, packed around the Palais de Justice, all the
way back to the bridges . . . Fears of violent public reaction . . .
Second session of Tribunal begins today . . . it's all running
away, so fast, out of control, can nothing stop the shouting, the
cruelty, the madness . . . (*She throws the newspapers away.*) . . . If
Robespierre had one flicker of manhood in that powdered
stick of a body, I'd go to him, offer him myself, let him do
anything . . . but no. Oh Georges, is there hope? (*Turns to the*
Servant.) Go down on the street. Listen, come back and tell
me what people are saying . . . Go!

The **Servant** *runs off.*

Hope.

Scene Five

The Committee of Public Safety.

Saint-Just, Collot, Barère.

Barère   What does the President of the Tribunal write
about the second session?

Saint-Just   It was worse than the first. The prisoners
demanded that certain members of the Convention and the
Committee of Public Safety appear. They appealed to the
people on the grounds that witnesses were being withheld.
The emotion was indescribable. Danton was like a parody of
Jupiter, roaring and shaking his locks.

Collot   All the better for Samson to grab hold of them.

Barère   We had better lie low. The scum on the streets, the
fishwives and bone men, won't be impressed by the sight of us.

Collot   The people relish being crushed, even by Danton just staring at them. The insolence of it. His face is more vicious than an aristocrat's coat of arms, an emblem of sneering contempt for humanity. A face that anyone who hates being looked down upon should want to smash.

Barère   He's cast himself as a hero. The blood of the September victims makes him invulnerable. What does Robespierre say?

Saint-Just   Nothing. He seems about to speak, but doesn't. The jury must announce they have all the evidence they need and end the debate.

Barère   Impossible.

Saint-Just   They must be destroyed! Even if we have to throttle them with our own bare hands. Dare! Dare! Danton taught us that word, we must be true to it. The Revolution won't stumble over their corpses, but if Danton stays alive he'll grab her by the skirt . . . Something in that man's face tells me he'd rape liberty herself to stay alive.

Saint-Just *is called out of the room. He is seen in a corridor giving money to a* **Gaoler** *from the prison. The* **Gaoler** *hands him something.*

Barère *looks at a paper.*

Collot (*takes a piece of paper*)   This woman writes a petition. Very personal terms.

Barère   One more forced to choose between the planks of the guillotine or the bed of a Jacobin?

Collot   She's too old for that. Madame begs for death. And eloquently: she says prison lies on her like the coffin's lid. She's only been there four weeks! (*He writes and reads out.*) 'Madame, you have not longed for death long enough.'

Barère   Collot, the guillotine must not become the butt of jokes. The people will lose their fear of it. We must not be familiar.

Saint-Just *returns holding up a paper.*

Saint-Just   I have just received a denunciation. There is a conspiracy in the prisons. The Girondin General Dillon got drunk in his cell and talked to a gaoler. The patriot reported the plot.

Collot   People have cut their throats on a bottle before.

Saint-Just   The plot is that the wives of Danton and Camille will throw the people money. Dillon is to escape, free the prisoners and, with them, storm the Convention.

Barère   But Dillon hates the Dantonists, how would he know their wives?

Collot   We know Danton has money squirreled away, from his war profiteering. The wife could use it.

Barère   No no, this is a fairytale.

Saint-Just   But a fairytale to send them to sleep. Evidence of treason!

Barère   But not real.

Saint-Just   The treason is real! Add to that the insolence of the accused, the discontent of the people, the confusion of the jury and . . . I'll write an official report.

Barère   Do that, Saint-Just, spin your sentences. Every comma the cut of a sabre, every full stop a severed head.

Saint-Just   The Convention must issue a decree that the Tribunal will continue its hearings without interruptions. And that any of the accused who act in contempt of the court or create a disturbance will be excluded.

Barère   You have the revolutionary's tactical instinct. A moderate demand to achieve an extreme effect. They can't be silent, Danton will have to cry out.

Saint-Just   I count on your support. There are those in the Convention who grow as diseased as Danton. They fear the same remedy. Their courage has returned, they are certain to protest against the flouting of procedure . . .

Collot   Go, Saint-Just! The lava of revolution flows. Liberty will strangle in her embrace those weaklings who dreamt of impregnating her mighty womb. The people will appear in thunder and lightning, like Jupiter, and burn them to ash. Go, Saint-Just, we will hurl down the thunderbolt upon the cowards' heads.

Saint-Just *goes off.*

Barère   Did you hear the word 'remedy'? Now they're making the guillotine a cure for the pox. They're not fighting the moderates, they're fighting vice.

Collot   We've gone along with it. So far.

Barère   But Robespierre wants to make the Revolution a lecture hall for morality. He uses the guillotine as a pulpit.

Collot   Or a prayer stool. Let him put his head on it, not his knees.

Barère   Anything can happen now. The world is topsy-turvy. Virtue turns murderer, criminals die like saints.

Collot   When are you coming to the whorehouse at Clichy again?

Barère   When the doctor says I'm in the clear.

Collot   Yes, you must think there's a comet over that place, flashing down rays of mercury, shrivelling your spinal column.

Barère (*shrugs his shoulders*)   Yes yes. But sh, the Incorruptible mustn't know.

Collot   He's an impotent Mahomet.

Collot *goes off.*

Barère   You monster. 'You have not longed for death long enough', the words should have severed your tongue as you spoke them.

Do I now rush in amongst the assassins of the Committee of Public Safety and grab the blade of the guillotine?

Why not? We are all prisoners at the feet of assassins, murdering each other. And if it is moral to kill one to save your life, why not two? Or three? Where does it end? Huh. I'm like a child playing with barleycorns. One, two, three, four, how many to make a pile? Come my conscience, come little chick, chick-chick-chick, here's food for you.

Scene Six

The Conciergerie.

Danton, Lacroix, Hérault, Philippeau, Camille.

Lacroix   You roared wonderfully, Danton. If you'd strained yourself like that earlier, we'd not be in this state now. But death makes you yell, eh? Coming closer and closer to your face till you smell his foul breath.

Camille   If only he'd just do it, mug you, rape you, tear the life out of your warm body in one last bitter struggle! But not like this, with all the formalities.

Danton   Yes. I wish it were a fight, tooth and nail. But I've fallen into a mill, my limbs are being ground off, systematically. I am being killed by a cold, mechanical power.

Hérault   Don't worry, my friends. Think of the autumn crocuses, that don't bear seeds till winter's gone. We're like flowers being transplanted, except when it's done to us we tend to stink a bit.

Danton   Huh. An edifying prospect: to be moved from one dung heap to the next.

Lacroix   So what do you want?

Danton   Peace.

Lacroix   Peace is in God.

Danton   No, it's in nothingness. But I am an atheist. And I believe atheism's cursèd argument: that nothing that exists can cease to exist. Flesh decays in earth, from earth springs new life. Something cannot become nothing. And the agony is: I am something.

Creation has spread itself so wide there is nowhere left empty. Everything swarms and seethes. The void has murdered itself, creation is its wound, we are its drops of blood, the world is the grave in which it rots. Crazy, what am I arguing? But there's a truth in there.

Camille   The world is the wandering Jew, it can never die. 'Oh pain of endless life', as the song says.

Danton   We're Pharaohs buried alive in three or four-layered coffins: the sky, our houses, our shirts and our jackets.

Life's just a more complex, a more ordered putrefaction than the simple rotting of death. But that's the only difference: complexity. Otherwise life and death are one and the same.

Still, I've got used to decay in life, I don't want to cope with the other sort. Julie. To die without her. Even if I am utterly destroyed, powdered into a handful of martyred dust, without her not one atom will have peace. I can't die. No, I can't die. I'll cry out. Let them wring every last drop of blood from me.

Scene Seven

A room.

Herman, Collot, Barère, Saint-Just.

Herman I don't know what to do. Danton and the others are out of control. Now they are demanding a commission of enquiry.

Collot I think this will get the bastards. The Committee of Public Safety's response: an emergency decree. (*He shows* **Herman** *a paper.*)

Barère Get them off our necks, and their necks, well, off.

Herman Yes yes. Just what we need.

Saint-Just Let's do it. End it now. For us and for them. (*Turns away.*)

Scene Eight

The Revolutionary Tribunal.

Danton The Republic is in danger and the President of the Tribunal has no brief! We appeal to the people. My voice is still strong. I will speak a funeral oration over the Committee of Public Safety. I repeat: we demand a commission of enquiry. We have important disclosures to make. I will withdraw into the fortress of reason. I will unleash the cannons of truth and crush my enemies.

Signs of applause. Enter **Collot, Barère** *and armed* **Guards.** **Saint-Just** *lurks where the* **Prisoners** *cannot see him.*

Herman Silence in the name of the Republic! The Convention has issued the following decree.

Collot (*reads the paper*) In consideration of signs of mutiny in the prisons; in consideration that the wives of Danton and Camille Desmoulins throw money to the people; in consideration of a conspiracy to lead insurgents to free the accused; and, finally in consideration that the accused have created disturbances designed to bring the Tribunal into disrepute, the Tribunal is hereby empowered to continue its investigations without interruption and with the removal of any of the accused from the court who try to speak.

Danton   I ask you, have we said one thing in contempt of the Tribunal, or the people, or the Convention?

Many Voices   No! No!

Camille   The bastards. They want to murder my wife.

Danton   One day men will know the truth. I see a great disaster overwhelming France. It is dictatorship, it has torn off its veil, it holds its head high, it tramples over corpses. (*Points at* **Barère** *and* **Collot**.) There they are, the murdering cowards, look at the ravens of the Committee of Public Safety.

I accuse Robespierre, Saint-Just and their executioners of high treason.

They want to choke the Republic in blood. The ruts made by the tumbrils are the highways on which foreign armies will flood the heart of France.

For how long must the footprints of liberty be graves?

You want bread, they throw you heads. You are thirsty, they make you lick the steps of the guillotine.

Violent commotion, shouts and applause.

Many Voices   Long live Danton, down with Robespierre!

The **Prisoners** *are forcibly removed. Uproar amongst the public.*

Many Voices (*chanting*)   Danton! Danton! Danton!

1st Citizen   Danton was with us on the 10th of August and when we beheaded the king, Danton was with us in September when we attacked the prisons. Where were his accusers?

Saint-Just *steps forward to the edge of the crowd. They do not recognise him at first.*

Saint-Just   Lafayette was with you at Versailles and yet he was a traitor.

2ⁿᵈ Citizen   Who says Danton is a traitor?

Saint-Just   Robespierre.

3ʳᵈ Citizen   Robespierre is a traitor.

Saint-Just   Who says so?

1ˢᵗ Citizen   Danton.

Saint-Just (*steps forward*)   Danton has fine clothes, Danton has a fine house, Danton has a fine wife, Danton bathes in Burgundy, eats venison off silver plates, Danton sleeps with your wives and daughters when he's drunk.

Danton was poor like you, where did he get it all?

– The King gave it to him, to save his crown.

– The Duke of Orléans bribed him to steal the throne for him.

– The foreigners gave it to him to betray you all.

– What's Robespierre got? Nothing but virtue. Virtuous Robespierre! You all know him

They back away from **Saint-Just**. *Hesitant then ferocious chanting.*

All   Long live Robespierre! Down with Danton! Down with the traitor!

Act Four

Scene One

A room.

Julie, a **Servant**.

Julie It's over. They trembled before him. Now they're killing him out of fear. Go, I've seen him for the last time. I don't want to see him like that.

*She gives the **Servant** a lock of hair.*

There. Take him that and tell him he won't go alone. He'll understand. Then come back quickly, I want to read his look in your eyes.

Scene Two

The Conciergerie. **Lacroix**, **Hérault** (*on a bed*), **Danton**, **Camille** (*on another*).

Lacroix Your hair! It gets so long. And your nails . . . it makes you ashamed.

Philippeau Don't sneeze. Dust gets in my eyes.

Lacroix And no one kick my feet. I've got corns.

Hérault And lice.

Lacroix It's not the lice I think about, it's the worms.

Hérault Well with that thought, goodnight. Sleep well friends. Lacroix, please don't tug at this corpse's winding sheet. It's cold.

Danton So, Camille. Tomorrow we'll be worn-out shoes, thrown to that old beggar woman, the earth.

Camille Nothing but the leather slippers Plato said the angels patter round the earth in. Oh Lucile!

Danton   Stop worrying, boy.

Camille   They can't touch her. The earth won't dare bury her, it'll form an arch over her, the vapours of the grave will sparkle on her eyelashes like dew, crystals will grow like flowers on her lovely skin . . .

Danton   Stop, stop. Sh, boy, sleep now.

Camille   Danton. Tell me. Secretly. Dying's just pain, isn't it? It achieves nothing. I want my eyes open, I want to stare straight into life's bright eyes, just a little longer.

Danton   Your eyes'll be open, like it or not. The executioner doesn't bother to close eyelids. Sleep is more merciful. Try to get some.

Camille   Yes. Lucile. A dream. Safe inside.

Danton   Will the clock never stop? With each tick the walls close in on me, narrow as a coffin. I read a story like that when I was a child. My hair stood on end.

When I was a child. All that effort to feed and clothe me, keep me warm, just to make work for gravediggers. I feel I'm already stinking. Dear body, I'll hold my nose and pretend you're a woman, warm, sweaty from dancing, and whisper to you. We had some times, body, you and I.

Tomorrow you'll be a broken fiddle, your tune played out. An empty bottle, the wine drunk. But lucky people who can still get drunk! A crumpled pair of trousers you'll be, body, thrown in the wardrobe. The moths will eat you up. Huh, this doesn't do any good. Yes, dying is pain. Death apes birth. We go to it naked and helpless babies. We get a winding sheet for swaddling clothes, but what comfort that? We whimper in the grave as we did in the cradle. Camille? Asleep. (*As he leans over him.*) His eyelids flicker. A dream. The golden dew of sleep.

He rises and goes towards the window.

Thank you, Julie. I won't go alone. But I'd like to have died differently. Effortlessly, the way a star falls, a note of music ends, a ray of light is lost in clear water.

The stars prick the night like tears. There must be great grief in the eye that shed them.

Camille   Oh! (*He has sat up and is groping toward the roof.*)

Danton   Camille, what's wrong?

Camille   Oh, oh . . .

Danton (*shakes him*)   Do you want to tear the ceiling down?

Camille   You! Speak!

Danton   You're shivering and sweating.

Camille   It's you. Me. My hand. I know where I am. Danton, the roof disappeared. The moon sank down right to my face. Heaven itself had fallen on my face. I hammered at it, I scratched at the stars. I was a drowning man, under a roof of ice . . .

Danton   The lamp throws a round reflection on the ceiling. That's what you saw.

Camille   Takes just that does it. To lose the little sanity you have . . . (*He stands.*) I won't sleep any more. I don't want to go mad.

He picks up a book.

Danton   What's that?

Camille   Young's 'Night Thoughts'.

Danton   Huh. You want a literary death before the real thing? Me, I'll read Voltaire's 'The Virgin'. I'm not slipping away from life out of a church confessional. I'll do it falling out of bed with a merciful sister in my arms. Life is a whore, who does it with all the world.

Scene Three

The square in front of the Conciergerie.

Lucile, *on a stone beneath the* **Prisoners'** *window.*

Lucile   Camille, Camille! (**Camille** *appears at the window.*)
Camille, you look so funny! You've got a whole stone
building on for a coat! And that iron mask on your face,
and where are your arms? Come on, fly down here. Listen,
I'll make you.

(*Sings.*)

> Two stars in the sky
> Brighter than the moon
> One at the window one at the door
> Of my true love's room.

Sh. Come on. They're asleep. Up the stairs. I've been
waiting here so long, alone with the moon. But you can't get
in the door! Wearing stones. Stones. Bars. Stop it, it's a cruel
joke, wearing those horrible heavy clothes. You're not even
moving. Why don't you speak? You frighten me.

Listen to me! Don't pull that face, long door-with-locks face.
Death has a long face. Death. What word's that, Camille?
Oh look, it's there. Hey, Hey, I'll catch it. Help me. Come,
come, come . . .

She runs off.

Camille (*calls*)   Lucile! Lucile!

Scene Four

The Conciergerie. **Danton**, **Camille**, **Hérault**, **Lacroix**.

Danton   I'm leaving everything in a terrible mess.

Camille (*to himself*)   There was madness in her eyes.

Danton   Who'll be left who knows anything about
government? They might get by if I leave Robespierre my
whores. And he decides to use them.

Camille (*to himself*)   But many are mad now, that's the way
the world's going. What can we do about it? Nothing.

Lacroix   They say we made Liberty a whore.

Danton   Which it always was!

Camille (*to himself*)   Heaven send Lucile sweet delusions. The greatest delusion is reason itself.

Lacroix   I look forward to the fools shouting 'Long live the Republic' as we go by.

Danton   What does it matter? Let the storm of the Revolution wash up our corpses where it will.

Lacroix   Robespierre is a Nero. Look how friendly he was to Camille just before he had him arrested.

Camille   Yes yes, but what do I care?

Danton   When history comes to open our tombs, despots will choke on the stench of our corpses.

Hérault   We stank pretty high in our lives too. You're talking to posterity, Danton, not to us at all.

Camille   All that wasted effort, pursing your lips, painting your face, putting on a good accent. We should take off our masks for once. Then we'll see, like in a hall of mirrors, only the infinitely repeated, age-old image of the fool, the joker's head. We are very like each other. All villains and angels, idiots and geniuses, all things in one. We all sleep, digest food, make children, we're all variations in different keys on the same tune. That's why we strut about and put on faces, we embarrass one another because we know each other so well. Spare yourselves the trouble. We all know each other.

Hérault   Yes, Camille, let's shout and scream.

Danton   Yes, why sit there tight-lipped in pain?

Hérault   Yes, Greeks and Gods screamed aloud, Romans and stoics pulled heroic faces.

Danton   Greek or Roman, they were all Epicureans. Like all of us, they did what made them feel good. Why rip ourselves to pieces over this? What's it matter if we hide our private parts with codpieces of laurel leaves and rose garlands, or just leave the horrid thing bare to be licked by dogs?

Lacroix   My friends, to God the clashes and cries of humanity that deafen us are a torrent of harmonies.

Danton   Oh, so what are we, poor musicians whose bodies make the music of the brutal world? Hideous sounds that drift up to die as a sensual breath in heavenly ears?

Hérault   Are the flames that roast us in history's furnace only feathers of light, that the Gods tickle us with to enjoy our laughter?

Camille   Is the universe a goldfish bowl, set on a table before the blessed Gods so they can laugh at us as we die?

Danton   The world is chaos. It will give birth to a God called 'Nothingness'.

The **Warder** *enters.*

Warder   Gentlemen. Your carriages await you.

Scene Five

A room. **Julie**.

Julie   People were running in the street. Now it's quiet. I won't keep him waiting.

She takes out a phial.

Dear priest. Your amen sends us to bed.

She goes to the window.

It's lovely to say goodbye. I've only to pull the door behind me.

She drinks.

I'd like to stand here, always. The sun's gone. The earth stood out so sharply in the light. Now it's still as a grave. The earth is a dying woman. The light is beautiful on her face.

She grows paler and paler.

She drifts, her clothes are heavy, spread wide. Will no one pull her from the stream and bury her? Sh. I'll go. Not a kiss, not a breath to wake her.

Sleep. Sleep.

She dies.

Scene Six

The Place de la Révolution. The guillotine.

Camille   Gentlemen, I'll be carved first. It's a classical feast. We recline in our places and spill a little blood, as a libation. Goodbye, Danton.

He ascends the scaffold.

*The **Prisoners** follow him, one after another.*

Danton *goes last.*

Lacroix   The tyrants will break their necks on the edge of my grave.

Hérault (*to **Danton***)   Pompous ass. He thinks his corpse will be a compost heap to ferment liberty.

Danton   Adieu my friend. Death is the best doctor.

Hérault (*tries to embrace **Danton***)   I can't joke any more, it's time.

Danton (*to the public*)   Citizens! I apologise to God and to man for creating the Revolutionary Tribunal. Which has destroyed so many and now destroys me.

*An **Executioner** pushes him back.*

Danton (*to the **Executioner***)   Will you be crueller than death? Will you stop our heads kissing in the basket?

End

Printed in the USA
CPSIA information can be obtained
at www.ICGtesting.com
LVHW020939171024
794056LV00003B/866

9 781408 132838